Outward Holiness

Carla Burton

DEDICATION

To my daughter, Caitlin, who is my biggest fan and my greatest legacy. Thank you for taking hold of the holiness given to you by your mother and your grandmother!

Inward holiness will produce *outward fruits*

but *outward holiness* will be

THE EVIDENCE OF *INWARD CHANGE*!

Contents

Chapter 1

Outward Holiness

Outward *after* Inward

Holiness has an order, and it must be obeyed in that order. First, we must have the right attitude concerning holiness. Having the right attitude throughout the process of holiness will be the key to our outward holiness being acceptable in the sight of God. Once we have the correct attitude, we must then understand the principles of holiness laid out in the Word of God. The principles help us to understand why holiness is important to God, and they give us guidelines to help us when we face issues of holiness in modern times. Living by principles based on the Word of God is a very safe and protected position.

After obtaining a right attitude and gaining an understanding of God's principles, we can begin to develop standards of holiness in our lives. Inward holiness must be present before true outward holiness can be attained.[1] Inward holiness is keeping a right spirit, a renewed mind, a guarded tongue, and having love for and unity with one another. These things are matters of the inward man, and God desires that our inward parts be holy before Him.

What God Sees

The final step of holiness is our outward appearance. Many people want to misuse the scripture in I Samuel 16:7 that says *"for the LORD seeth not as man seeth; for man looketh on the outward appearance, but the LORD looketh on the heart"* to mean that God is not concerned with our outward appearance. The setting of this scripture is Samuel's mission to anoint a new king in Israel. His eye was caught by the beauty of Eliab, the son of Jesse, and he assumed that Eliab was surely the anointed of the Lord. That is when the Lord made Samuel aware that He was looking for different qualifications in the next king of Israel.

God *is* concerned with our outward appearance. Our outward appearance is a separation from the world, and it is our witness of the inward change God has made in our lives when He fills us with His Spirit. The Lord shows us the importance of outward holiness in Matthew 23:25-26 when He criticizes the religious leaders of the day: *"Woe unto you, scribes and Pharisees, hypocrites! for ye make clean the outside of the cup and of the platter, but within they are full of extortion and excess. Thou blind Pharisee, cleanse*

---

[1] See *Steps to Holiness* and *Inward Holiness* by Carla Burton for more information on the order of holiness.

*first that which is within the cup and platter, **that the outside of them may be clean also**.*" Yes, the condition of the inside of a person is very important to God, but Jesus lets us know that inward holiness is what helps us clean up our outside appearance. We wouldn't wash the inside of a plate and cup without taking time to make sure the outside was clean also. We must make sure that our outward man is involved in the process of holiness along with our inward man.

A Nightstick, a Measuring Stick, and a Walking Stick

During my research and prayer concerning this subject I felt the Lord gave me an analogy between holiness and sticks. We use holiness as three different sticks -- a nightstick, a measuring stick, and walking stick.

A nightstick is used primarily for law enforcement. Police officers use it to subdue or beat down someone who is committing an offense. As Christians, we often use holiness as a nightstick to force people to submit to our beliefs. A nightstick is never viewed in a positive manner by its victim. It is simply a tool to inflict pain and keep a person in line with a set of rules.

A measuring stick is only as good as the measurement you assign. The only person who knows the measurement is the person with the stick. Many times we use outward holiness as a measuring stick. If someone doesn't measure up to our expectations, or measurements, then they are not holy in our sight. Jesus told us to first get the beam from our eye before working on the splinter in someone else's

(Luke 6:41-42). He was telling us to be careful about pulling out our holiness measuring sticks and using them on each other.

The purpose of a walking stick is to help balance a person. This is the kind of holiness we need to emulate and strive to produce. Holiness in our lives is to bring balance so that we can please God and be accepted into His presence. A walking stick can only benefit someone else if the person with the stick has balance. We cannot help someone else produce holiness unless we are first following the entire process of holiness. I want to have a walking stick holiness so that it can produce balance in my life and then I, in turn, can help others find balance in their lives.

A Godly Principle Passed Down

One of my greatest concerns is when I hear this upcoming generation say that they don't believe that some of the outward holiness standards, that we have held fast to for so many years, are "important" anymore. I am not blind to the fact that culture is different and that perhaps there are a few things that due to the advancement of this age have morphed overtime to reflect more modernization. However, those always need to be weighed against the underlying principle from the Word of God before changing. And example of this might be regarding the topic of television. Many years ago TV was a unit in your home with rabbit ears that brought in no more than 4 channels. So we could preach against having these in our homes and allowing them to steal our time and distract our attention from God. However, due to the advent of so much technology we have had to adjust our viewpoint because now the box is not just in a home, but most people carry access to this on their cellphones or tablets. So preaching against the "box" is not wise nor does it maintain the underlying Biblical principle that we need to be teaching. The principle is that we "make a covenant with our eyes" as Job stated and not "put any wicked thing before our eyes". If we live our lives by this principle then it doesn't matter where the box is – we will always make sure we are being obedient to outward holiness in our lives. So I strongly push basing all your outward holiness standards on Biblical principles that surpass time and culture.

With that said, I do feel that this generation has to be extremely careful that we are not using culture to move us away from the principles of the Word of God. In the Old Testament we see the story of Moses at the burning bush. Exodus 3:3-5 relates this story but I am drawn to verse 5, *"And he said, Draw not nigh hither: put off thy shoes from off thy feet; for the place whereon thou standest is holy ground."* God began right at this moment to teach Moses a lesson regarding holiness, standards and His presence. Remember in earlier chapters I told you that holiness is all about access to the presence of God. The more of this world that you put off the more access to God's presence you can experience. The mount Sinai example used earlier in this book explains this concept. Moses could ascend to the top of the mountain because he had learned the principle of putting off something to have more access to the presence of God. He learned that here in Exodus 3. God showed Moses that outward holiness is important to Him because God chose an item of clothing for Moses to remove as a symbol that he was willing to be cleansed so that he could approach God.

Then came the day that Moses passed off the scene and the next pastor stepped up. God anointed Joshua to become the leader and pastor of Israel. Joshua is ready to begin the greatest period of revival and growth for Israel. But before this takes place God wants to be sure that the new generation still lives by the principle established in the previous generation. In Joshua 5:13-15 we see the story of Joshua standing at the precipice of his greatest victory – Jericho. He lifts up his eyes and sees a man standing with a sword drawn. Joshua walks over to him and asks, *"Art thou for us, or for our adversaries?"* The angel responds by basically saying, *"Neither, I'm on the Lord's side".* What a reflection of holiness because holiness is NOT ABOUT YOU – it is about His Kingdom, His Presence and His Power.

In verse 15 God speaks to Joshua and asks him to do something. *"Loose thy shoe from off thy foot; for the place whereon thou standest is holy."* Almost the exact same wording that God shared with the previous pastor, Moses. God is showing us that even though there may be a new leader, a new territory to claim, a new level to reach – the way into His presence will NEVER CHANGE! You have to make sure that you still know the formula to have access to His presence.

This is my greatest concern when I see men and women around me that have been raised under the "burning bush" principle of holiness and access to God. But then I see them begin to move away stating that they don't "feel" or "think" that this is important any more. When I look back at two of the greatest leaders of the Bible – Moses & Joshua – they each lead at different times, different eras, gained different territory and worked with different people but they lived under the same principle of the purpose and vision of holiness – access to God!

Perspectives

To truly understand and explain outward holiness in this day and age, we have to look at it from three perspectives.

First, what does the Bible teach concerning the issue? The Bible is our foundation of beliefs, and it's very important that we are able to back things up with the Word of God. During my days in Bible school, a theology teacher explained it this way: where the Bible speaks, you speak; where the Bible is silent, you be silent. We must have the Word to back up our beliefs.

Second, we must look at history. We must understand how our culture has changed, particularly in the past decade. What were the motivating factors that cause us to believe certain things are okay today when a little over 100 years ago they were wrong? We have to dig below the surface to see how our worldly culture has affected our standards of holiness.

Third, we must take principles found in the Scripture and our culture's history into account when making up a standard for living holy in modern times.

We'll look at several areas of holiness using these perspectives in this study. I trust that when you have finished this booklet, you will have a better understanding and a deeper appreciation for dedicating yourself to God through outward holiness.

Outward Holiness

Chapter 2

Why Standards?

Wordless Conversations

Our outward appearance is not only a reflection of our inward condition, but it also identifies who we are. When we walk through the mall, we have a conversation with everyone we pass, and we never say a word! What you wear says something about who you are and what you believe in. The world acknowledges this fact by placing certain people into easily identifiable uniforms. For instance, policemen, firefighters, doctors, athletic teams, prisoners, etc. wear clothes that identify them as such. Even though the world wants to tell us that we can be independent in our dress, their actions say something else entirely. We identify people and pass judgment on their beliefs according to their outward appearance.

Modest Apparel

In Genesis 38 the Bible tells a story of a woman who deceived her father-in-law simply by changing her manner of dress. The story shows us that even then people were identified by the way they dressed. Judah thought that his own daughter-in-law, Tamar, was a prostitute simply by how she was dressed. *"When Judah saw her, he thought her to be an harlot; because she had covered her face"* (verse 15). Proverbs 7:10 also mentions the *"attire of an harlot."* We cannot say that what we wear is not important when even the world identifies it as important.

In I Timothy 2:9-10 the scriptures says, *"In like manner also, that women adorn themselves in modest apparel, with shamefacedness and sobriety; not with broided hair, or gold, or pearls, or costly array; But (which becometh women professing godliness) with good works."* The word "modest" here is the Greek word kosmios, which means well orderly and proper. How we dress and behave says a lot about who we are as women. We profess godliness (or that we are trying to be like Him), yet our appearance denies the fact that we are His. We must understand that what we wear identifies whom we belong to. Genesis 1:27 says, *"So God created man in his own image in the image of God he created him; male and female he created them."* We were created to reflect the image of God. The way that He created us is the way that He desires to see us. There is distinction in dress and gender. Genesis specifically tells us that we were created beautiful and that there is a difference between male and female. We are identified as His by the way we adorn ourselves outwardly.

Principle Versus Positional Standards

Earlier in this book, we discussed the importance of principles. And we understand that there are many areas in which the Bible is extremely clear that this is not a suggestion but rather a commandment with a principle attached to it. The same applies in the Christian Discipleship area of holiness. There are certain holiness standards, which have a very clear and defined spiritual principle attached to them. And as we are obedient to these standards we release the principle in our lives.

But there are some holiness standards that do not have a clear, defined spiritual principle attached to them. Rather, as we study these standards throughout the Bible, we see them as positional standards. In other words, as people moved their position closer to God, they applied these standards to their lives. When they moved away from God, they would go back and pick up these things. This is why we call these positional standards.

When looking at the standards found in the Word of God, we see that there are two that have very clear defined spiritual principles applied to them; clothing and hair. When we obey in these areas we release the blessing of the spiritual principle. When we disobey we also release the curse of the spiritual principle in our lives.

There are other standards that the Word does not have a clear, defined spiritual principle applied to them. But as you read the Biblical accounts of them, you realize that these were positional standards. When God desired His people to be closer to Him, He would request them to remove these items. When the people would grow cold in the Lord, they would go back and pick up these items. So even though there is not a direct, clear spiritual principle applied to these standards, it does not mean they are not important. They show, outwardly, the condition of our spiritual relationship and commitment to God. They show our position with Him.

The Goose & The Gander

You know that old saying, "What's good for the goose is good for the gander". Basically saying that men and women both must do the same thing. In the Apostolic world, however, I have often heard the comment that there seems to be a lot of standards for women and not as many for men. I disagree with this. As you read through the standards in the next few chapters, you will see that every one of them is to be applied in obedience in both genders. There may be a different application but there should be the same obedience to the principles and positional standards asked of us by God.

When we talked about spiritual principles above we noted that there were two standards that had definite spiritual principles applied to them; clothing and hair. These are the same for both men and women – but in different applications. This means that there is a standard for clothing and hair for men and women. They are each expected to participate in the standard so that the spiritual principle will be applied and the attached blessing or curse will be released in their lives.

Carla Burton

Chapter 3

Separation by Clothing

The Biblical Perspective

To understand the spiritual principle of clothing, you have to travel all the way back to the Garden of Eden. Genesis 1:27, *"So God created man in his own image, in the image of God created he him; male and female created he them."* Immediately, we see a spiritual principle born, there will be two distinct gender roles and these roles will be defined in everything; in their bodies, in how they dress and in their purpose.

The spiritual principle behind our clothing is that we maintain a distinction between men and women. When we look at the actions of the world in changing how men and women dress, we can step back and see the spiritual principle motivating all this change. Satan does not have original ideas of his own. His only purpose is to present his twist on the ideas (commandments) of God. And the only thing he can do is get us to agree to cross gender lines in our dress and then he gets us to disobey the spiritual principle. When you see the spiritual principle attached and you understand the tactics of the enemy, you can then look beyond culture and the influence of the fashion industry. They are simply carrying out the wishes of the enemy without truly understanding the spiritual principle behind their actions.

Even the world subconsciously admits that there is a spiritual principle attached to this standard. They do things without even realizing that the DNA that God created in them is making this choice. Every bathroom door across America has two symbols, one representing male and one representing female. The male symbol is a man in pants; the female symbol is a woman wearing a triangular skirt. So even in America they still define women and men by clothing. And they define men's clothing as trousers or pants and women's clothing as a skirt.

We see this continued when we study the homosexual world. Whenever you see them together, one will take on the masculine role and one will take on the feminine role. If homosexuality is just about being able to love someone, then why do they go back and adapt to the original gender roles? Because it is a spiritual principle created into their DNA, and no matter how they try and bypass the letter of the law they will never be able to change the spirit of the principle. Their heart and spirit will always try and recreate these roles, because it tells them that this is innately correct. No matter the action, the spiritual principle shines through.

In Deuteronomy 22:5 the Lord shares His desire for the sexes to remain separate in dress by saying, *"The woman shall not wear that which pertaineth unto a man, neither shall a man put on a woman's garment: for all that do so are abomination unto the*

LORD thy God." The key to understanding this verse is the word "pertaineth." Many people today want to tell us that there are "women's" pants or other items that are specifically made for women. But the Lord said it this way so that we could realize that once again He is stressing the distinction of the sexes. In our culture there is one item of clothing that is strictly male and that is pants or trousers. The only type of man who would wear a dress in our culture is a transvestite. Ordinary men would never dream of putting on a dress or skirt. So we can say that any type of pants is an item of clothing pertaining to a man. God asked women to abstain from wearing those garments, which pertain to the male gender so that we can be distinctive in our dress. Remember that holiness is about being pleasing to God. The last part of this verse tells us that when we don't dress distinctively according to our sex, we actually become an abomination in His sight. I have often asked people how they feel when they see a male transvestite. I know that I am completely disgusted or become almost sick to my stomach to see that kind of perversion. But the scripture plainly tells us that God views a woman who dresses as a man in the same way. They make Him sick to His stomach. We don't need to justify the way we dress; we just need to obey the Word of God and remain female in our dress.

One of the most powerful scriptures in the Bible concerning holiness is found in Romans 12:1-2. *"I beseech you therefore, brethren, by the mercies of God, that ye present your bodies a living sacrifice, holy, acceptable unto God, which is your reasonable service. And be not conformed to this world: but be ye transformed by the renewing of your mind, that ye may prove what is that good, and acceptable, and perfect, will of God."* The scripture clearly states that we must present our entire bodies unto the Lord as holy. It cannot only be our inward parts, but it must be our outward appearance as well. In verse 2, Paul tells us that we are to be "transformed," not "conformed," to this world. When a person becomes a Christian, he or she should not conform to the standards of this world which tell us how to live, how to dress, and how to look. We should be transformed completely. To be transformed is to be completely changed! To do a 180 degree turn and change who we are. Many people "accept Christ," but they are never inwardly or outwardly transformed. When you really become a Christian, you will change in your outward appearance as well as your inward appearance.

Our Culture's Perspective

Even our culture acknowledges the distinction between male and female. The definition of the word "trousers" in the dictionary shows that the garment is distinctively men's clothing. It is defined in Webster's Revised Unabridged Dictionary (©1996, 1998 MICRA, Inc.) as "a garment worn by men and boys, extending from the waist to the knee or to the ankle, and covering each leg separately." Many people want to say that pants or trousers are female clothing, but culturally and by definition, they are men's clothing.

We even use phrases to denote the fact that pants are a sign of gender and authority. We ask, "Who wears the pants in that family?" We associate pants with the male or leadership role in the family. We cannot say that clothing doesn't define what gender role we are trying to play.

The Historical Perspective

If you need anymore convincing, let's look at the history of trousers. How did we get to the point where pants are an acceptable piece of clothing for women? What were the influencing factors in this change in culture? Remember that Paul tells us in Romans to be transformed or changed, not to conform to the culture around us.

The idea of wearing split pants came directly from the Women's Liberation Movement. The women who started this movement were all extremely liberal in their thinking and very opposed to submission to men or to the Bible. In the 1700's the leader of the movement was Mary Wollstonecraft. She wrote a book entitled, A Vindication of the Rights of Woman in 1792. She rebelled against all the moral and decent laws of that day, even living with a man and giving birth to a child out of wedlock. Then in the 1800's, two women stepped forward to try to push the women's movement even farther. Lucretia Mott and Elizabeth Cady Stanton were both greatly opposed to the Bible, especially on the subject of divorce. In fact, Elizabeth Cady Stanton wrote a paper in which she says, "I rejoice over every slave that escapes from a discordant marriage." On July 19, 1848, the first Women's Rights Convention was held in Seneca Falls, New York. It was only two years later, in 1850, that women began to wear trousers (at that time called bloomers) underneath shortened dresses.

Amelia Bloomer, a feminist editor, was the first to start this trend, thus the name "bloomers." Even Ms. Bloomer in her magazine, The Lily, said in 1851 that she hoped "female readers will not be shocked by her appearance or that her male readers would not mistake her for a man." This was quoted beneath a cartoon rendering of her in her "bloomers." What the power of the printed word could not do, the power of the visual aid could. Amelia Bloomer could not change the course of history just through a few cartoon drawings, but with the advent of the movie industry in the 1920's, our culture took a dramatic turn.

In the 1920's, three things took place that began our blurring of the gender lines. First was World Wars I and II. Men went to war and women had to step into their jobs. As women began to take on more and more of the male role in society, their dress began to change as well. Second was a renewal of the Women's Rights Movement that took place around that time. Women began to realize that if they were going to take on the men's responsibilities in the workplace, they wanted the men's rights as well. Last was advent of the movie industry.

One of the greatest influential figures of the 1920's and 1930's was an actress by the name of Marlene Dietrich. She was a self-proclaimed bi-sexual and her favorite item to wear was a man's double breasted pants suit. She was also one of the most famous actresses of that day. Once America began this diet of war, women's rights, and movies, it wasn't long until they began imitating what they were seeing. In 1939, women began to openly wear slacks. In January 1955 the state of California passed a law giving women the right to wear trousers to work.

From the advent of the movie industry in the 1920's, we can see the rapid downward progression of clothing. In 1925 short skirts began to appear. For the first time a woman would show her ankle and calf -- something that had never been done before. In 1939 women began to wear slacks. In 1960 we were introduced to the miniskirt, pants suits, hot pants, and short shorts. The designers of the 1960's said they were striving to make "uni-sex" clothing -- in other words, clothing that could be worn by either sex. Through the next decades we have seen clothing drastically change. Today clothing has been so gender-blurred that it is hard to tell a man from a woman many times.

As women have taken the male gender roles, men have stepped back into the female gender roles. Men today wear earrings, they grow their hair long, and they wear multiple rings and necklaces. Often times it is hard to determine the gender of people when their backs are turned to us.

We must be careful that we are pleasing to God in our dress. Not only must we dress in the gender role that He created us in, but we must be careful to maintain our modesty in our clothing. I once heard it asked, "If Jesus walked into the room would you be comfortable dressed as you are?" This is a question that we need to ask ourselves each time we get dressed. God desires us to remain in the role He created for us and to be careful that we glorify Him in our dress.

Here is a summary of our standard of dress through the biblical and historical perspectives. In Genesis 1:27, God set up a principle. He created us to maintain our distinction as male and female. He commands us in Deuteronomy 22:5 to make sure that we are dressing based on our gender. The apostle Paul tells us in I Timothy 2:9 to dress modestly to be pleasing to God. Historically, our concept of what is acceptable for a man to wear and for a woman to wear has been influenced by ungodly groups and social movements. The truth of the matter has not changed; our culture still uses pants to identify males and skirts to identify women. We must conclude that women should abstain from wearing pants just as men should abstain from wearing skirts or dresses.

God tells us in I Peter to be holy because He is holy. We cannot follow after movies, the Women's Rights Movement, and other things that are not of God. These are Satan's tools to distract us and make our lives not pleasing unto God. We must develop a love for God and His ways so that we can overcome the world and its pressures.

Chapter 4

Separation By Hair

The Biblical Perspective

First we must establish what the entire concept of hair is about. It is not simply about having long hair on a woman or short hair on a man, but it is actually about a very important concept from the Bible – submission to authority. That is why the entire scripture setting for the discussion on hair begins with Paul saying in I Corinthians 11:3, *"But I would have you know, that the head of every man is Christ, and the head of the woman is the man; and the head of Christ is God."* Paul is very clear at the beginning of the issue concerning hair that this is about submission to the chain of authority established by God. When a woman remains in submission to her head, the man, there are blessings and protection that follows. You will see later on when we discuss the history of hair that the movement came out of a spirit of rebellion. Women did not want to remain in their God-ordained position and so began the process of cutting that authority. Many women will say that when they cut their hair they feel that they have been freed from a bondage that they felt in before. Do I believe that they really feel a spirit of freedom? Yes! But it is a spiritual feeling, not just an emotional or physical feeling. When they cut their hair, they actually step out of their role as a woman and into the man's position of authority. Of course our flesh loves this feeling. It is the same feeling that Satan wanted when he desired to step out of submission to authority in heaven. Isaiah 14:12-15 describes how Satan desired to be lifted up and become equal to God. In Galatians 5:19, we see the works of the flesh being laid out. In Galatians 5:20 we see one of the works of the flesh is "emulations," which means "to be equal to." That was the spirit that Satan exhibited in Isaiah when he desired to be equal to God. That is the same spirit that will come upon us when we step out of our specified role in submission to authority.

Not only is the condition of our hair a sign of our submission to authority, but it also places us once again in obedience to Genesis 1:27 where the Lord created us distinctly male and female. As we look through I Corinthians 11 we will see that our hair defines us our physical role as well. There are basic laws in nature that define what is male and what is female.

Paul's instructions on hair begin with the order that God created for authority. The man is the head of the woman, and as such he must be in his place of submission to God, his head, for a woman to remain in her proper place. In I Corinthians 11:4 Paul says, *"Every man praying or prophesying, having his head covered, dishonoureth his head."* Paul is telling the men that if you pray or prophesy while your hair is uncut then you have not only dishonored your physical head but your spiritual head as well. The spiritual head of the man is Christ. When a man tries to pray to God while his hair is uncut, he is actually telling God that he is not interested in remaining submitted to His authority. Children who are completely rebellious to parents usually wind up in trouble. We must remember that if we want all the promises, blessings, and protection that God has for us we must remain submitted to His authority.

There should be no debate about whether Paul is speaking of cutting or not cutting the hair when he uses the word "covering." The next scripture clarifies the meaning of a covering. I Corinthians 11:5-6 states, *"But every woman that prayeth or prophesyeth with her head uncovered dishonoureth her head: for that is even all one as if she were shaven. For if the woman be not covered, let her also be shorn: but if it be a shame for a woman to be shorn or shaven, let her be covered."* Paul clearly shows us that the word "cover" refers to the woman's hair being uncut. It is not the length of hair that God is concerned with; it is the condition of the hair being cut or uncut. Women of different race and culture may have hair that only grows to a certain length while others may have hair that can grow to enormously long lengths. God did not specify a certain length to be in submission to authority. He simply says He is looking for cut versus uncut! If I took hair that was extremely long and cut off approximately one inch, we would probably agree that the hair was still long in length. If I cut off another two inches, we would probably still say it was long. The question is, when does is it become short? In God's eyes it became short the instant it was cut. This is very important for us to understand or we can try and justify why we do certain things. Don't justify trimming your hair by saying that it's still long. According to I Corinthians 11:5-6, if you cut your hair, then in the sight of God you should just go ahead and shave it all off.

During the Bible days if someone had their hair shaved off, it was a shame and embarrassment to them. In Isaiah 3:24, Isaiah prophesies the fall of Judah. He tells them that because of their rebellion towards God, He will cause a scab to come upon the crown of the heads of the daughters of Zion (verse 17). Instead of "well set hair," there will be baldness. We must truly understand and obey the scripture concerning our proper place of authority and the condition of our hair. When a woman prays or teaches with her head uncovered, or cut, then she dishonors not only her physical head but her spiritual head, the man, as well. We could dedicate an entire book to the subject of the importance of submission to authority. However, let me say that if you desire peace, contentment, happiness, joy, strength, the promise of health, long life, a great marriage, children who are in submission to your own authority, power with God, power over the enemy, all the promises in the Word of God, and financial peace in your life, then a woman must remain in submission to her husband and through him to God. In Jeremiah 7:28-29, Jeremiah prophesies to Judah concerning the nation's disobedience. He says because they disobeyed the voice of the Lord (or rebelled), they should just cut off their hair and throw it away. His prophesy refers to Judah and Israel as women who are a shame to Him, so the evidence of their rebellion would be the cutting of their hair. It is very important that women show that they are submitted to the authority in their lives by not cutting their hair and men do the same by cutting their hair.

In I Corinthians 11:7-9, Paul gives us an understanding of Genesis 1:27 and why we were created distinctly male and female. *"For a man indeed ought not to cover his head, forasmuch as he is the image and glory of God: but the woman is the glory of the man."* Once again Paul restates that man should have his hair cut because he is created in the image of God and should reflect His glory. Genesis 1:26 states that God created man in his likeness or image. We are the only creation on earth that is made like He is in heaven. God intends for a man to show forth His glory and power by maintaining his male defined status. Then in Genesis 2:21-23, God created woman. Paul restates the order of authority by saying that the woman is the glory of the man. Woman was created from the man's body, so she was created to walk beside a man to help him and reflect his glory. In other words, what I do represents my husband. I Corinthians 11:8-9 states, *"For the man is not of the woman; but the woman of the man. Neither was the man created for the woman; but the woman for the man."* We know this statement is true because of Genesis. God created the man for His glory and then created the woman from the man for the man's glory. This is the order of God and no matter how much you want to kick against it, you will never change His spiritual and physical order.

However, the Lord gave women some power as well. In the Garden of Eden the serpent came to the woman and caused her to sin first. But the Lord, understanding Eve's fall from grace, also gave her a special place in subjecting Satan. First, in Genesis 3:15, God promises Satan that the seed of a woman (prophesying the birth of Jesus) will bruise his head. Satan would bruise the heel of the seed (prophesying the death of Jesus on Calvary) but then the seed would bruise the head of Satan (the resurrection of Jesus Christ). Then in I Corinthians 11:10 Paul states, *"For this cause ought the woman to have power on her head because of the angels."* If a woman remains in submission to God's chain of authority (God-man-woman) by not cutting her hair, then she becomes a curse to Satan. Remember that his fall was all about rebellion to authority, and when we remain submitted to authority, we bring new condemnation upon his kingdom. Each time I worship in church with my hair uncut, I again condemn Satan for his fall from heaven, his temptation of Eve, and his rebellion against God. I am also a sign to the angels that remain in heaven about the joy that is in a submitted life. I am glad to know that each day I can condemn the devil and witness to the angels just through my submission to authority.

In I Corinthians 11:11-12, Paul tells the man and woman that they need each other for the chain of authority to continue correctly. *"Nevertheless neither is the man without the woman, neither the woman without the man, in the Lord. For as the woman is of the man, even so is the man also by the woman; but all things of God."* God has a divine purpose for men and women, but we have to remain in our proper place in the chain of authority for our purpose to be fulfilled. God created us to need each other and to work together to build a family and the kingdom of God. He lets us know that He created all things, but He created them to work together in the proper order. In the spiritual world the man and the woman need each other to make it all work. Also in the physical world, the woman would never have existed except God created her from man; neither would men exist in the world today without a woman to give birth to them. We depend on each other for our very existence, so why would we not subject ourselves to God's order?

In the next few scriptures Paul talks about what nature teaches us. I Corinthians 11:13-15 states, *"Judge in yourselves: is it comely that woman pray unto God uncovered? Does not even nature itself teach you, that, if a man have long hair, it is a shame unto him? But if a woman have long hair, it is a glory to her: for her hair is given her for a covering."* Paul wraps up this entire sermon about hair with a statement on our natural inclinations concerning hair. When we see two people walking with their backs turned towards us, both with long hair, our first thought is "women." Many times I have been shocked to realize that one or both of them were men. We instinctively view long hair as being a female attribute and short hair as a male attribute. It is not that we are trained that way, but God created that nature within us. Likewise women who have really short hair can be mistake for men at times. Our hair is our glory, and it represents our covering in the chain of God's authority. We must make sure that we are obedient to the Word of God. In I Corinthians 11:2, Paul refers to the way we keep our hair as ordinances or laws. He is instructing us on how to be pleasing to God and maintain our relationship with Him.

One of my greatest frustrations as a pastor's wife is the abuse of I Corinthians 11:16. Many people use this scripture to justify cutting their hair. It states: *"But if any man seem to be contentious, we have no such custom, neither the churches of God."* Some people want to interpret this scripture to mean that if anyone has a problem with Paul's instructions concerning our hair, just do what you want to do. I don't see where in any of Paul's other writings, he would give a sermon on how to live correctly and then seem to change his mind. God did not have Paul write I Corinthians 11:1-15 and then in verse 16 tell us that if we don't agree with him, just toss out verses 1-15. My Bible says that God does not change! The interpretation of this scripture is simply this. If anyone wants to argue about this issue just tell them this is how Christians live and do things. The greatest translation that I have ever seen of this scripture is found in The Promise Bible: Contemporary English Version (Thomas Nelson, Publisher). It says, *"This is how things are done in all of God's churches, and that's why none of you should argue about what I have said."* It is not an "out" to do what you want; in fact, it is just the opposite. Paul says this is how we live as Christians so just quit arguing and obey the Word of God!

The Historical Perspective

The cutting of women's hair began with the advent of the movie industry and the Women's Rights Movement in the 1920's. During this era when the men were going to war and the women were taking on the men's jobs, women went into barber shops and asked for a "bob." The term "bob" was used because it changed a woman's hair from looking female to looking male, and they used a man's name for the haircut. Men didn't even know how to cut women's hair, so they would simply cut it straight along the bottom and straight above the eyes. That is the traditional "bob" cut. At the same time that women began cutting their hair, they also began to shorten their skirts, tear out the sleeves (the first sleeveless dresses), and add much ornamentation (bangles and fringe in gold and silver) to the hem, neckline, and sleeves of the dress. Look at dresses during the flapper era. The cutting of the hair came from the Women's Liberation Movement. Isn't it amazing that they would call it "liberation" when that was exactly what they were doing? They were liberating themselves from submission to God's chain of authority. Don't get confused; you can feel a great spirit of liberty when you cut ties with God. But that is just temporary. When you need God's mercy, God's protection, and God's promises, that's when that liberty becomes your curse. It is better to stay submitted to God now and have access to all of His Word. An amazing statistic is that in 1922 there were 5,000 beauty shops, and in the next two years there were 23,000. By the year 1924, 70% of all women in New York had bobbed their hair.

If you still don't believe that hair is a sign of a woman's submission to God, let me take you to the 1960's. Even modern historians agree that this was the age of rebellion. People rebelled against the law, against the war, against government, against their parents and against all morality and decency of that day (the Sexual Revolution). During this time we saw an amazing trend. Women cut their hair extremely short. In fact the most famous woman's haircut of that day was the pixie cut. It was cut so short that there was no hair below the back of the neck. At the same time that women were cutting their hair to look like men, men were growing their hair out as a sign of rebellion. The look of the 60's for men was hair below the shoulder blades, unkempt, with long sideburns and mustaches. These people didn't even understand that they were rebelling against a spiritual precept.

Here are some reasons why we obey I Corinthians 11:1-16:

1. It is a sign of our submission to the chain of God's authority;

2. It demonstrates a wife's submission to her husband and then to God;

3. It demonstrates a husband's submission to God;

4. It is a sign upon the head of a woman to the angels to remain in submission to God's authority;

5. It is a condemnation to Satan and his angels that we remain in good standing with God because of our submission;

6. It continues the distinction that God set up in Genesis 1:27 of male and female;

7. It is shameful for a man to approach God in prayer with uncut hair;

8. It is a glory for a woman to approach God with her hair uncut;

9. Nature teaches us what is right; and

10. As long as we remain in submission to God we have access to all the promises given us in the Word of God.

Chapter 5

Modern *Media*

Satan's Tools

The greatest tool that Satan has ever had is modern media. It has been the single most effective cultural thermostat there is. The difference between a thermometer and a thermostat is that a thermometer simply measures the temperature, but the thermostat actually sets the temperature. Television, movies, magazines, books, and radio have radically changed the culture in which we live today. Every day the devil blasts his message through every media. We cannot enter a store without hearing his music or seeing his message. Our children, our teens, and our adults are desensitized by the bombarding messages of premarital sex, homosexuality, violence, and self-gratification. It is vital that we keep our hearts right with God and limit our intake of media. Job 31:1 explains it best by saying, *"I made a covenant with mine eyes...."*

I would ask you the question "Is sin in technology?" What is worse -- a television or a telephone? Technology is not the problem; the problem is the heart of man. Look at Eve. She committed the first sin, and she didn't even have a television, a telephone, or a Cosmopolitan magazine! If your heart is wicked, you will find a way to sin with or without technology. Many churches don't have televisions; however, they have telephones that are used for gossip and tearing down the church. Man has been sinning from the beginning before any technology was available.

We must make a choice to commit ourselves to the Lord completely and subject our flesh to what we know is right. We must guard our hearts, minds, ears, and eyes from sin that is made accessible to us via all types of media: telephone, television, computer, magazines, and books. One is no worse than another, and all can be abused. Remember that change begins inwardly but produces outward fruit.

In Psalm 101:3, David says, *"I will set no wicked thing before mine eyes: I hate the work of them that turn aside; it shall not cleave to me."* The term "wicked" is interpreted in the Hebrew to mean "thing of Belial or Satan." I don't think we have to watch television, be on a computer, pick up a magazine, or open a book to understand that these can be Satan's tools. He uses these things to promote his ideology and doctrine. The apostle Paul was very clear on what we should be focusing our mind. In Philippians 4:8

he instructs us, *"Finally, brethren, whatsoever things are true, whatsoever things are honest, whatsoever things are just, whatsoever things are pure, whatsoever things are lovely, whatsoever things are of good report; if there be any virtue, and if there be any praise, think on these things."* Our job is to keep our mind under control and subjected to the Spirit of God.

In Psalm 119:37 David prays, *"Turn away mine eyes from beholding vanity...."* I need the help of the Lord in my life to be able to overcome the influence of this world. Isaiah explained that by guarding our eyes and ears we could actually dwell in the presence of God, have a strong defense, be sustained with bread, and be sure. Isaiah 33:15-16 states, *"He that walketh righteously, and speaketh uprightly; he that despiseth the gain of oppressions, that shaketh his hands from holding of bribes, that stoppeth his ears from hearing of blood, and shutteth his eyes from seeing evil; He shall dwell on high: his place of defence shall be the munitions of rocks: bread shall be given him; his waters shall be sure."* This scripture indicates that we make the choice to participate in or to abstain from these evils.

There are many media outlets that we could participate in and perhaps would not be sin; however, in everything we do we are a witness of God. I Thessalonians 5:22 tells us to abstain from the very "appearance of evil." I believe that we must be careful that our witness does not receive irreparable damage from our actions.

The condition of our inward man is reflected in our outward man. In Matthew 15:18-20 and Mark 7:21-23, Jesus explains that things from within come out and defile us. Here's a list of items that He says come from within an unguarded heart and proceed out: "evil thoughts, murders, adulteries, fornications, thefts, false witness, [and] blasphemies." It's like reading the latest movie script from Hollywood. We must be wiser than a serpent and understand that all these things are simply tools for Satan to plant his ideology in the hearts and minds of men. If he can get a person full of these sinful ideas, then that person will eventually produce those ideas outwardly. Proverbs 23:7 confirms that "as a man thinking in his heart, so is he."

The world understands the power of what we see. That is why we have sayings like, "the eyes are the windows of the soul" and "a picture is worth a thousand words." We can see the power of what we see in the coverage of World War I and II and the Gulf and Iraqi Wars. Modern America can see each battle as if they are there via television, magazines, and the Internet instead of waiting months to see a grainy, black and white photo of what is happening on the other side of the world. We are bombarded each day with images, and we must make sure that we are following Paul's advice about absorbing information that is true, honest, pure, lovely, and of a good report!

Radio, Television, and Film

Let's take a look at the history of radio, television, and movies. Each was created with a good intention -- improving communication. They were intended to bring people from all around the world closer together by being able to communicate faster and clearer. Radio was used to tell America that Japan had bombed Pearl Harbor, television sent the first images of a man walking on the moon, and even documentary films have shared the images of Nazi death camps during World War II.

Television was first seen at the 1939 World Fair, but regularly broadcasted programming did not begin until the 1940's. At first, no one thought television would be that big of a deal, but quickly people began to change their minds. In the 1950's the teachers, parents, and social scientists put out a statement warning against the violence that could be seen on TV. I'm amazed that there was such concern about the possible effects of television during the 1950's. I wonder what those same people would say about the programming on television today.

Our society has become so consumed by this media. The following are just a few alarming statistics concerning television:

1. During the elementary years of a child, they will have seen over 20,000 murders and 80,000 other assaults.

2. By the time a student graduates high school they will have spent 11,000 hours in school and 15,000 hours watching TV.

3. Students who are heavy TV watchers (four or more hours per day) are poor readers, bad students, don't play well with friends, have fewer hobbies and activities and are more likely to be overweight.

4. 20 to 25 violent acts will be committed every hour on Saturday morning "children's programs."

5. TV has shortened our attention spans.

6. TV is a thief of time. The average person watches 50,000 to 75,000 hours of TV in his lifetime. That's 5-8 years of his life spent in front of a tube.

Social scientists have identified three effects of

television violence on viewers:

1. They become less sensitive to pain and suffering in others;
2. They are more fearful of the world around them; and
3. They are more aggressive and more likely to harm others.

Television is sending an immoral message to our children today. It says that homosexuality is just another lifestyle and can even be funny. It leaves out the horrors of AIDS and the loneliness of the homosexual lifestyle. And yet this is one of the most popular causes promoted by actors and sitcoms. Slowly and surely television is desensitizing our children to the consequences of the homosexual lifestyle.

The media in general advocates pre-marital sex (fornication) and teaches our children that it is okay and safe. It is taught in school and through the media that there are no consequences for fornicating. It makes those who remain pure seem not normal and weird. Every night on television there are numerous people engaging in this behavior. What example do we want our children to follow? We must control their intake of television and movies, as well as other media such as magazines and books.

The media tells us that adultery and multiple relationships are part of a normal life. It doesn't expose the emotional damage adultery produces in a marriage and in the lives of the children involved. Instead it gives awards to soap opera stars who have been married nine times or more on their shows. We must see the danger of allowing our lives to be consumed by this ideology.

The key to all media is the heart. Your pastor cannot

write laws of holiness in your heart. He can control what is on his platform at church, but if your heart is determined to do evil, then you will. Be like Job and make a covenant with your eyes. Love God enough to focus on good things and abstain from evil things. I believe that every Christian needs to control what they see and hear through television, the telephone, the computer, movies, books, and magazines. If you are absorbing too much of the world and not the Word, then you need to clean up your act and get your heart right with God.

Chapter 6

Make-Up

The Biblical Perspective

The Bible tells us in Genesis 1 that we were made in the image of God. We were created to reflect to the world His image and His glory. Everything we do in our outward appearance reflects either His image or an image of the world. We must continually look at each aspect of our outward image and make sure that we are shining forth His true light.

In the Bible, a woman painting her face is noted as a harlot or a prostitute. A woman would paint her face or eyelids specifically to attract attention and entice someone. Never in the Bible does a woman paint her face to entice the presence of the Lord. In fact, in I Peter 3:3 the Bible says, *"Whose adorning let it not be that outward adorning of plaiting the hair, and of wearing of gold, or of putting on of apparel; But let it be the hidden man of the heart, in that which is not corruptible, even the ornament of a meek and quiet spirit, which is in the sight of God of great price."* The purpose of make-up is to alter a person's appearance to entice someone. It is a tool to draw attention to ourselves simply for the sake of vanity. We must make sure that we are being careful to desire only the attention of God on our lives and be pleasing to Him.

In II Kings 9:30, Jezebel painted her face to try to entice Jehu and keep him from killing her. Somewhere in Jezebel's life this ploy had worked before, and here she was trying it again. In Proverbs 6:24-26, the Bible speaks of the adulteress and not allowing her to "take you with her eyes." It lets us know that this woman was trying to destroy something precious by enticing someone with her looks. Jeremiah 4:30 says, *"And when thou art spoiled, what wilt thou do? Though thou clothest thyself with crimson, though thou deckest thee with ornaments of gold, though thou rentest thy face with painting, in vain shalt thou make thyself fair; thy lovers will despise thee, they will seek thy life."* The person of whom Jeremiah speaks painted her face and tried to make herself beautiful for her lovers. Read Ezekial 23:40-49. The painting of the eyes is used to describe Israel and Judah as two adulterous sisters. In the Bible the Lord always uses make-up in conjunction with the sin of lust. Remember the purpose of holiness is to be accepted into His presence and to be holy as He is holy.

In the book of Esther, a young Jewish girl is among the candidates chosen to be the new queen. She endures separation from family, a year long purification process, and then it is time for her to go in unto the king. Esther 2:13 tells us that as each maiden's turn comes to go in to see the king, she is given the opportunity to choose whatever adornment she wanted or felt she

---

[2] *Matthew Henry's Commentary on the Whole Bible: New Modern Edition, Electronic Database. Copyright © 1991 by Hendrickson Publishers, Inc.*

needed. In Esther 2:15 the Bible tells us that Esther "required nothing" before approaching the king. Matthew Henry's commentary 2 states it this way:

She was not solicitous, as the rest of the maidens were, to set herself off with artificial beauty; she required nothing but just what was appointed for her (v. 15) and yet she was most acceptable. The more natural beauty is the more agreeable.

This story is a great analogy of holiness. Esther's whole objective was to be pleasing and accepted by the king. Our responsibility is to be pleasing and accepted by our King. He created us as we are, and we need to be careful not to pick up the ideas of the world on beauty. David acknowledged the perfection of God's creation in Psalm 13:13-16:

For you created my inmost being; you knit me together in my mother's womb. I praise you because I am fearfully and wonderfully made; your works are wonderful, I know that full well. My frame was not hidden from you when I was made in the secret place. When I was woven together in the depths of the earth, your eyes saw my unformed body. All the days ordained for me were written in your book before one of them came to be. (NIV)

God made us and knows how well we are made! We are each beautiful and wonderfully made before Him. We must seek to draw His attention through our meek and gentle spirit, our praise and worship, and our love of being holy as He is holy. We should avoid using the outward trappings of the world to become its idea of beauty.

The Historical Perspective

In the 1920's when the movie industry began, all pictures were in black and white. So to be able to make the actresses' and actors' faces stand out, they had to apply enormous amounts of make-up. One actress in particular was famous for introducing the practice of wearing make-up off the set and into public. Her name was Theda Bara and her nickname was "Vampire." She was given this name not as it relates to the story of Dracula, but because she was said to seduce and destroy men on screen. Movie theaters were packed each night to watch her "vamp" another young man. She influenced women of that day to throw moral caution to the wind, paint their faces with extreme make-up and go out on the town for a night of "vamping."

Any Christian should be able to understand that this is not an influence that we should follow. We should reflect the morals of Christ and not the world.

The original use of make-up dates back to Egyptian times. A heavy, dark make-up, called "kohl" was used to outline the tops and bottoms of the eyelids. Any woman made up in this manner signaled to men that she was a prostitute and available.

In the Bible, Egypt was a type of the world and sin and slavery. After experiencing God's freedom, why would anyone want to remain in bondage to the world and sin? God separates us to be His witness and His people just as He did the children of Israel.

Realize that the spirit of make-up is not from God. It indicates a spirit of lust and adultery according to the Word of God. The use of make-up comes from a long history of prostitution and, in the more recent past, the movie industry. God made us in His image and desires for our appearance to reflect His glory at all times. It is important that we understand the motivating factors behind an issue and determine whether or not it is good for us to be involved in that issue. Make-up has become a tool Satan uses to convince women, in particular, that they are not beautiful as God created them. We must be careful not to fall into his trap of worldly ideology. Let our appearance reflect the glory of God completely.

Carla Burton

Chapter 7

Jewelry

The Biblical Perspective

Our motivation for doing the things we do to our appearance is a great issue with God. I Samuel 16:7 shows us that He knows our hearts and what motivates us. The outward beauty of Jesse's sons impressed Samuel but not God; God was concerned more with the condition of the heart of a man and how it reflected Him outwardly.

Throughout the Bible we see many references to jewelry; however, anytime God wanted His people to draw closer to Him or be more consecrated to Him, He asked them to remove their jewelry. In Genesis 35:1-7, God desires Jacob to draw closer to Him, so Jacob makes some changes in his camp.

And God said unto Jacob, Arise, go up to Bethel, and dwell there: and make there an altar unto God, that appeared unto thee when thou fleddest from the face of Esau thy brother.

Then Jacob said unto his household, and to all that were with him, Put away the strange gods that are among you, and be clean, and change your garments:

And let us arise, and go up to Bethel; and I will make there an altar unto God, who answered me in the day of my distress, and was with me in the way which I went.

And they gave unto Jacob all the strange gods which were in their hand, and all their earrings which were in their ears; and Jacob hid them under the oak which was by Shechem.

And they journeyed: and the terror of God was upon the cities that were round about them, and they did not pursue after the sons of Jacob.

So Jacob came to Luz, which is in the land of Canaan, that is, Bethel, he and all the people that were with him.

And he built there an altar, and called the place El-beth-el: because there God appeared unto him, when he fled from the face of his brother.

God wanted Jacob to build Him an altar or a place where He could commune with (or be closer to) Jacob. The people took off those things which represented the world and went into the presence of the Lord clean. So our first conclusion concerning jewelry is that putting it off helps us to draw closer to the presence of God. In Romans 12:1, Paul tells us to "present our bodies, a living sacrifice, holy, acceptable unto God." Holiness is taking our body and making it acceptable to the presence of the Lord. He desires us to put off some things so that we can be allowed into His presence.

In the first booklet of this series on holiness, Steps to Holiness, I related the story of the children of Israel at the foot of Mt. Sinai. The Lord tells Moses that the people are not allowed to even touch the mountain where His presence is being displayed in thunder and lightening. Exodus 19:18-25 is the story of God telling Moses not to allow the people into His presence. The Lord lets Moses know in verse 22 that the people needed to be "sanctified" or cleansed before they could come into His presence.

Exodus 11 relates the story of the children of Israel leaving Egypt. The Lord instructs them in Exodus 11:2 to collect gold, silver, and jewelry from all their Egyptian neighbors.

First of all, notice that jewelry began in Egypt. The Israelites borrowed the jewelry from the Egyptians -- not the other way around. You never see in the scripture where the Lord tells them to wear the jewelry. In fact, this jewelry causes them to get in trouble in Exodus 32:1-4. The very jewelry that they brought out of the land of Egypt, which was symbolic of them winning a war and spoiling their enemy, they melted into an idol to worship. The main reason that the Lord wanted them to take the jewelry was to make the items needed for worship in the wilderness tabernacle. In Exodus 35:22, they brought all their jewelry to be used to build the tabernacle.

In Judges 8:24, the wearing of earrings identified people as Ishmaelites. Ishmael was the son of Abraham with Hagar, Sarah's Egyptian handmaiden. Ishmael was not the promised son, Isaac, but was actually the disobedience of Abraham and Sarah. Instead of waiting on God to fulfill His promise to them, they took the promise into their own hands. Today we still reap the pain of this decision because the dissention between the Israelites (children of Isaac) and the Arab nations (children of Ishmael) continues to affect our lives.

When Gideon asked the children of Israel in Judges 8:24-27 to give him the earrings of their prey, it wasn't for a good reason. In fact we see that his obtaining this jewelry caused him to sin, and in turn, he caused Israel to sin. Once again the people wearing the jewelry were not the children of God, but they were actually known as the children of the world by the jewelry they wore. Our responsibility in holiness is to reflect the image of God.

We are identified by what we wear. Others will know to whom we belong and whom we represent by what we wear. Jeremiah 4:30 not only speaks of make-up but also of the harlot that adorned herself with gold to attract the attention of many lovers. She was showing these men that she wasn't an ordinary woman, but was available for other uses. We must be careful because we can take the ornaments of the world and try to represent Christ. I Peter 3:3 tells us to not let our adorning be with the outward wearing of gold, but to let our appearance show that we represent Jesus Christ. Ezekiel 23:40 also tells the story of another harlot who adorned herself with ornaments meant to attract attention to herself.

In Hosea 2:13, the Lord gives a prophecy concerning Israel. He explains that in the days of Baalim, when Israel was turning away from Him, they did a few things. The woman to which He refers is Israel. She decked herself out with jewelry and went after other gods. She was playing a harlot and adulteress in the sight of God.

The Historical Perspective

In studying the history of jewelry, we don't really see many references to people wearing anything until the time of the Egyptians. Before that time it was mostly shells or rocks that people would wear around their necks or arms. Most jewelry that originally was worn was used to show that they worshipped a certain god. In Eypt the sun god, Ra, was worshipped by wearing a sunburst carved into gold on your arm, neck, or head. The Pharaoh and those of his household wore a lot of jewelry in the form of signet rings, wide collared necklaces that covered them down to their chests, golden crowns and head pieces, bracelets of gold around their upper arm and their lower wrist, and many other smaller types of jewelry. They wore these things to represent their personal wealth, their position above all the other people and as talismans to ward off evil.

Throughout the rest of history, through the ages of the Greeks, the Byzantine Empire, the development of Europe, the discovery of America and down to present times, jewelry has continued to be used to show wealth, power, and position. Henry VIII of England had the most opulent collection of jewelry. His daughter, Elizabeth I, loved wearing large amounts of jewelry all over her body. During this time there was a great separation between the rich aristocrats and the poor. It was also during this time that King Louis XIV of France and his queen, Marie Antoinette, caused the French Revolution due to their personal opulence while the rest of the country was so poor they could not eat.

Jewelry was also used as a tool to keep slaves bound together. They would create a necklace of steel, gold, or iron and place a ring in the front. They would create similar items for the wrist and feet. Then they would string the slaves together in a long line and make them walk. It was a way to make sure that no one escaped; however, if by chance someone got away everyone would know they were a slave by the necklace, bracelet, or anklet.

In the Bible Egypt is used as a type of sin or the world. When God brought the children of Israel out of Egypt, the first place He took them was to Mount Sinai to show them how they could be accepted into His presence. He was very specific that they were going to have to put off the patterns, styles, and conduct that they had learned while living in Egypt 400 years. When God saves us from this world there should be transformation in our lives according to Romans 12:2. We should not act, walk, talk, or look like what God saved us from. In Egypt the Israelites were bound together as slaves. They had no personal or religious freedom. They lived according to the dictates of Pharaoh and their Egyptian masters. God even told Moses and Aaron to tell Pharaoh to let His people go so they could "worship" Him in the wilderness. Obviously they had been hindered from truly "worshipping" God the way they wanted to in Egypt.

History shows us that the true start of jewelry came with the

Egyptian kingdom and was used as a way to worship all their gods. The one true and living God shows us through His Word that each time He wanted someone to draw closer to Him, He requested they take off their jewelry and other things that represented the world.

Finally, what is our motivation or purpose for wearing jewelry? That outward adornment is not for the eyes of God, but rather to attract the eyes of man. My purpose in this world is to be a witness of Him and show who I truly belong to. I want the world to look at me and see a difference. I want them to realize that I am transformed by the power of Jesus Christ. If you want to draw closer to the presence of God, then you will put off things that could stand in your way. It won't be a sacrifice to put those things down, but rather a privilege to come into His holy presence and commune with Him.

Carla Burton

Chapter 8

Tattoos & Piercings

The Biblical Perspective

Many years ago the inclusion of this topic in a book on holiness may not have been necessary, due to the fact that this was not prevalent in our society. However, when you look around and see the increase of people getting both tattoos and piercings, we have to define the Biblical standard and our cultural trend to be able to speak definitively on this topic.

Leviticus 19:28 says, *"Ye shall not make any cuttings in your flesh for the dead, nor print any marks upon you: I am the Lord."* Remember when God originally called Abraham, He asked that he come out from the people around him and be separate (different). The pagan people of that day used tattoos to try and appease the god's and get help for loved ones who had died. God had asked His people to not be like others and this was to keep them separated unto Him and for His glory. In fact, by keeping our bodies clean and unmarked, we show that we are truly His and belong to Him.

In 1 Corinthians 3:17 we also see the scripture underline this point regarding ownership of our bodies. *"If any many defile the temple of God, him shall God destroy; for the temple of God is holy, which temple ye are."* We would be horrified if we saw someone come into our church and begin to spray graffiti on the walls, but this is how God feels when we mark up His temple – our bodies. I Corinthians 6:19-20 continues to explain this by saying, *"What? Know ye not that your body is the temple of the Holy Ghost which is in you, which ye have of God, and ye are not your own? For ye are bought with a price: therefore glorify God in your body, and in your spirit, which are God's."* When you receive His Spirit you no longer belong to yourself but you have become His house, His temple, His dwelling place. Therefore remember that marking your body is defacing His property. He wants us to represent Him and be separate from the rest of the world.

The Historical Perspective

When you read about the history of tattooing you will realize that it always had some sort of spiritual reasoning behind it. Some of the first tattoos were seen on mummified bodies from Egypt. The tattoos represented markings for loved ones that were given to help the god's accept them into the afterlife. They were used as protection against evil spirits. They believed that if they were tattooed with a symbol of a diety (such as Ra – the sun god), then his enemies would not attack the person. People would be tattooed with the picture of an animal of that day because they believed that that animal would not attack them. Later on during the Greek and Roman eras, people were tattooed to denote them as slaves or criminals. Their crimes and names of their victims would be tattooed in a prominent location so that everyone that met them would know their crime and they could never hide what they had done. Slaves were tattooed so that they could never escape slavery but would always be known by their markings. Even during the time of the settlement of our West, the American Indians would use tattoos to show how many they had killed. Tattoos have been used as good luck charms, to prevent sickness by keeping evil spirits away and to denote their religious beliefs.

The history of piercings dates back also to the cultures of the Old Testament. They would pierce people to show ownership or property. They would require their wives to wear symbols of ownership and the bigger the item placed in either the nose or ear, denoted the wealth of the owner. The modern age of piercing began with the Punk music movement, which began at the end of the 1960's and the beginning of the 1970's. It was their symbol and they told people that it was to show their rebellion against conservative values. Even today, if we see someone with excessive piercings, our first thought is that they are rebellious. It is associated with this overall theme.

Our Perspective

When we look at the Bible and see that we do not belong to ourselves, but we are His temple (dwelling place), we make a choice to be unmarked to represent Him. Then we look at the fact that tattooing and piercing throughout history has always been a sign of pagan religious rituals, slavery and rebellion, then it is clear what our decision must be regarding this behavior.

The Bible also teaches us to take into account the end of things instead of just the beginning. We need to carefully consider how we will feel about what we are doing later on in life. Statistics say that 20-50% of people later in life regret getting a tattoo.

However, I don't think a discussion of this topic would be complete without addressing how we should treat those who are born again out of this world and already have tattoos. Due to the rise of the popularity of tattoos in our culture, we have to realize that we will have many people who will come to God and already have marked their bodies. We can often feel (our traditional values) uncomfortable to use these people in our churches. However, I always keep two things in mind when controlling my thoughts and actions about this. First of all, if God filled them with the Holy Ghost while marked, then I should be careful to not place my opinion higher than His. We can ask them to wear longer sleeves and try to cover as much as they can, but if they are committed, faithful and following Jesus, then we must overcome our own prejudices and issues and allow God to use them.

In Acts 15, a similar issue arose in the new church. Paul & Barnabas had come to share with the apostles in Jerusalem all the good things that had been happening among the Gentiles. While there, the Jewish church members begin to request that the Gentiles be circumcised so that they would be in agreement with Mosaic Law. However, Peter answered them in verses 7-11 by telling them that God had filled them with the same Holy Ghost without circumcision and therefore we should not put more on them that God would require of them.

Secondly, the Bible tells us that judgment begins at the house of God (1 Peter 4:17). This simply means that when someone comes in and is filled with the Holy Ghost, baptized in His name and walking in the Spirit, we have to cease judging them based on past actions or issues. We have to allow their new life to begin. We have to find a way to overcome our issues and allow them to begin anew.

It is easy to ask someone to get rid of their piercings, but tattoos are permanent and hard to get rid of. We do not need to make that a requirement of usefulness or service in the Kingdom of God. We can ask that they cover as much as they can, but we have to train ourselves and teach our people to be Biblical not only in our standard but in our judgment of others as well. If God has forgiven us our issues, which may not be visible but would be just as sinful, then we must forgive others their issues no matter where they manifest themselves.

Chapter 9

Standards are Our Protection

There are many standards that are set forth in the Word of God. They are given to us for our protection. They are not given to be a prison in our lives. God wants us to have access to everything He has written in the Bible, but we must maintain holiness so that we can be accepted into His presence.

The principle of submission to authority is one that is a theme throughout the Word of God. But we not only have to submit to the authority of the Word, but to our pastor and leadership as well. God has given us shepherds who are given the responsibility of teaching us the Word and helping us continue to walk with God. Many times issues arise that may not be sinful, but a pastor may set standards or boundaries for his flock with their best interest in mind. If our pastor gives us guidelines that we choose not to obey, then the problem is not the issue or standard, but our lack of submission to the authority God has placed in our lives. When a pastor draws a line regarding an issue, at that point every person in that church has to make a choice. They can submit to the admonishment of their pastor or continue to disobey his direction. If they choose to disobey the pastor, the Lord isn't concerned about the issue anymore; He is concerned about that person's rebellious attitude. Each church is different, and different pastors ask different things of us. The most important thing we must do is keep a submitted heart and attitude and allow God to deal with us in our lives.

I was once asked to speak to a group about dealing with holiness problems. My response was that I don't really have holiness problems in my church. Don't get me wrong, there are people who are not submitted to our church's holiness standards, but I don't have to deal with petty arguments and disagreements about holiness. I believe that the cure for holiness problems is proper holiness teaching. If we can get people to understand that the proper order for holiness is a right attitude, understanding God's principles, inward holiness, and then outward holiness, then we can solve a lot of the problems we face in our churches. Many problems are personal disagreements because we don't have the right attitude concerning holiness. I don't have to mediate between women or men in my church. I teach them that we are all in the process of holiness. I may be at mile marker 2,000 while someone else is just starting at mile marker 10. The only thing I am concerned about is the direction the person is moving. As long as the person is moving towards God, then we are okay. The instant that he or she starts moving away from God, we have a problem. I have always taught in our church that my job is to be behind my new converts, encouraging them in the process of holiness. My job is not be in their faces telling them what they do and don't need to do. I may become a stumbling block to them as they are trying to go towards God. However, if I am in my proper place (behind them, encouraging them) in holiness then if they happen to turn around and try to return to world, I can become a stumbling block to their backsliding. It is important that we submit to the Word of God, the authority and command of our pastor, and that we maintain the true order of holiness.

I am doing all that I can to fulfill I Peter 1:16, *"Because it is written: Be ye holy, for I am holy."* Read this holiness study and then teach this holiness study. Let's strive to be like Jesus.

Recommended Reading

Watkins, Penny. *A Hair Short of Glory.* Hazelwood, MO: Word Aflame Press, 1996.

Pamer, Nan. *I Will Not Bow.* Hazelwood, MO: Word Aflame Press, 1997.

Pamer, Nan. *Modesty.* Hazelwood, MO: Word Aflame Press, 1990.

Bernard, David. *In Search of Holiness.* Hazelwood, MO; Word Aflame Press, 1988

Made in the USA
Columbia, SC
18 January 2025

51193257R00043